Valentine's Day

Kathryn A. Imler

Heinemann Library
Chicago, Illinois

HEINEMANN-RAINTREE

TO ORDER:

☎ Phone Customer Service **888-454-2279**

💻 Visit **www.heinemannraintree.com** to browse our catalog and order online.

©2003, 2008 Heinemann-Raintree
an imprint of Capstone Global Library, LLC
Chicago, Illinois

Editorial: Rebecca Rissman
Design: Kimberly R. Miracle and Tony Miracle
Picture Research: Kathy Creech and Tracy Cummins
Production: Duncan Gilbert

Originated by Chroma Graphics (Overseas) Pte. Ltd
Printed and bound in China by South China Printing Co. Ltd.
The paper used to print this book comes from sustainable resources.

ISBN-13: 978-1-4329-1045-7 (hc)
ISBN-10: 1-4329-1045-0 (hc)
ISBN-13: 978-1-4329-1053-2 (pb)
ISBN-10: 1-4329-1053-1 (pb)

12
10 9 8 7 6 5 4 3

Library of Congress Cataloging-in-Publication Data
Imler, Kathryn A., 1950-
  Valentine's Day / Katheryn Imler
    p-cm. – (Holiday histories)
Summary: Presents background information on the origins and traditions of customs related to the celebration of St. Valentine's Day.
Includes bibliographical references and index.
  ISBN: 978-1-4329-1045-7 (HC) 978-1-4329-1053-2 (PB)
1. Valentine's Day—Juvenile literature. [1. Valentine's Day. 2. Holidays] I. Title. II. Series.
 GT4925.155 2003
 394.2618—dc22
                    2003007888

Acknowledgments
The author and publishers are grateful to the following for permission to reproduce copyright material: **p.4** ©James and James Photography/Jupiter Images; **p.5** ©Jose Luis Pelaez Inc/Getty Images; **pp.6, 7, 9, 11, 13, 15, 16** ©Hulton Archive/Getty Images; **p.10** ©akg images-London; **pp. 12, 17, 20, 21** ©North Wind Picture Archive; **P. 14** ©Richard Cummins/Corbis; **p.18** ©Mary Evans Picture Library; **p.19T** ©Bettmann/Corbis; **p.19B** ©KJ Historical/Corbis; **p.22, 23** ©American Antiquarian Society; **p.24** ©William Hart/Stone/Getty Images; **p.25** ©Ariel Skelley/Getty Images; **p.26** ©Burke/Triolo Productions/Food Pix/Getty Images; **p.27** ©The Bridgeman Art Library/Getty Images; **p.28** ©Rommel/Masterfile; **p.29** ©Jose Luis Pelaez, Inc./Corbis;

Cover photograph reproduced with the permission of ©Corbis/Jupiterimages/Brand X

Contents

Some words are shown in bold, **like this**. You can find out what they mean by looking in the glossary.

A Holiday About Love

Red hearts hang everywhere. People bake cookies and dust them with red sprinkles. Stickers and colored candy hearts say, "I love you."

It is Valentine's Day. People send pretty cards. They give flowers and candy to special friends. It is a special time when we can tell people how much we care for them. But where did this special day come from?

A Roman Festival

This is a drawing of a Roman chariot race.

Many people believe Valentine's Day began as a Roman **festival**. In ancient Rome, the first day of spring was February 15. The Romans held a festival to celebrate this. They sang songs, danced and had races.

This drawing shows Roman children playing at a festival.

The day before the festival, girls put their names on slips of paper. Boys drew the name of a girl from a bowl. She was his playmate for the festival. Sometimes they fell in love.

Who Were the Romans?

Long ago, there were people called Romans. The Romans came from Italy and spread into many other countries. These countries became known as the **Roman empire**.

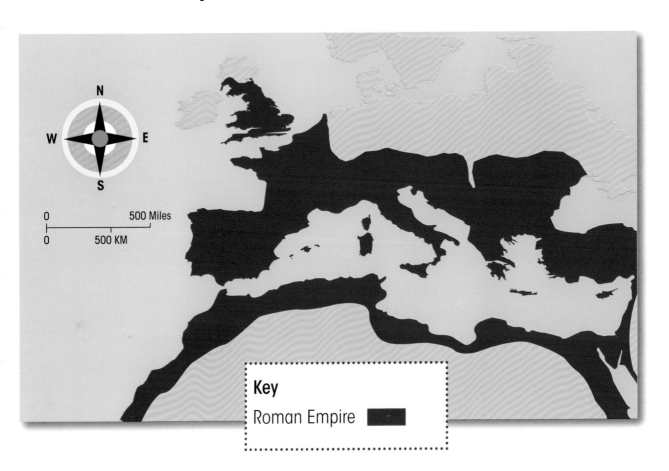

500 Miles

500 KM

Key

Roman Empire

During these times Rome was the greatest city in the Roman empire. **Emperors** ruled Rome. The emperor was a powerful man. He had control over many people.

An emperor was ruler of a large group of countries.

Emperor Claudius II

There was a Roman emperor named Claudius II. Claudius II wanted to protect his lands and people. It was important for him to have a big and strong army.

Claudius II wanted his soldiers to think about winning battles. He was afraid married men only thought about their families. So Claudius II **outlawed** marriages for young men.

A Man Named Valentine

A Catholic **priest** lived in Rome at this same time.
His name was Valentine. Some people believe
Valentine went against the emperor's law. They say
he secretly married young couples in love.

This picture shows Valentine being arrested.

Soon Emperor Claudius found out. He **arrested** Valentine and put him in jail. He had Valentine put to death on February 14.

Honoring St. Valentine

The Catholic Church tried to get Romans to be Catholic. They wanted them to give up their Roman gods. They wanted them to stop having their spring **festival**.

Later, **Pope Gelesius** I changed the festival. He made a new festival to honor the brave **priest** named Valentine. The Pope made February 14 St. Valentine's Day.

Early Customs

Over time, other countries started to celebrate Valentine's Day. Each one had its own **customs**. In France, fancy dances were held for young men and women.

In Italy, couples often walked through gardens together. Men read love poems to the ladies. Soft music was part of the celebration, too.

Valentine Cards

By 1600, many people in Europe were sending cards on February 14. The cards were called valentines. The English especially liked to send cards with love poems.

Very expensive valentines appeared in England. The queen of England liked fancy valentines with lots of ribbons and lace. Hearts, flowers and birds covered the cards.

Valentine's Day in the Colonies

In the 1700s, people from many different countries came to the colonies in America. They brought different **customs** with them. Many of them celebrated Valentine's Day.

In those days, towns were small. Sometimes people gave each other simple, handmade valentines. Sometimes they sent pretty cards.

Esther Howland

After the colonies became the United States people were very busy building the country. They only made a few homemade valentines. In the late 1800s, a woman named Esther Howland started making cards.

Many people wanted her to make their valentines. She hired people to help her make the valentines. By 1920, several companies were making cards for everyone.

MAKING VALENTINES.

Other Gifts

There are other ways to say, "Happy Valentine's Day." Anything shaped like a heart is a good gift. Some people bake cookies.

Sweet treats like candy are also nice. Some people give flowers. Red roses are very special.

The Symbols of Valentine's Day

Long ago, people believed that feelings like love came out of our hearts. Our hearts are red. Red became the **traditional** color for Valentine's Day. Red hearts became a big symbol for Valentine's Day.

Another symbol is **Cupid**. He looks like a baby boy
with wings and a bow and arrow. The legend says
whomever he shoots with his arrow will fall in love.

I Love You

Valentine's Day is a day to show people how important they are. It might be a friend, a parent, or a teacher. It might be someone who is lonely.

February 14 is a day for sweethearts. It has become a time to celebrate all kinds of friendships. Nothing is better than saying, "I love you."

Important Dates

Valentine's Day

Around 200 C.E.	Emperor Claudius II outlawed solidiers getting married
269 C.E.	Valentine is put to death
496	Pope Gelesius I named February 14 to be St. Valentine's Day
Around 1400s	Other counties began to celebrate Valentine's Day
1600s	People in England began to celebrate Valentine's Day
1700s	Valentine's Day is celebrated in the colonies
1847	Esther Howland became one of the first US manufacturers of Valentine cards

Glossary

arrested taken by the law (police)

custom usual way of doing something

expensive costing much money

fancy having lots of decoration

festival celebration

outlaw forbid

Pope Gelesius leader of the Catholic Church who declared February 14 Valentine's Day

priest religious leader

Roman empire group of lands controlled by the people in Rome, Italy from 100 C.E. to 476 C.E.

traditional way of doing something year after year

Find Out More

Bodden, Valerie. *Valentine's Day.* Mankato, MN: The Creative Company, 2005.
Trueit, Trudi Strain. *Valentine's Day.* New York: Scholastic, 2006.
Zocchi, Judy. *On Valentine's Day.* Sea Girt: NJ, Dingles & Company, 2005.

Index